know
the
game

GW00370636

# Gymkhanas

## Toni Webber

EP Publishing Limited

# CONTENTS

*Slicing lemons with a sabre is unlikely these days to be part of a village gymkhana's programme, but it was a fine test of skill during an army 'jolly' a century ago*

*Acknowledgements:* Photograph on this page by courtesy of Mary Evans Picture Library; cover photograph and photographs on pages 17, 18 and 20 by courtesy of Spectrum Colour Library, and on pages 27 and 29 by courtesy of Barnaby's Picture Library.

## HOW GYMKHANAS BEGAN

It all began in India in the nineteenth century. Nobody knows who organised the first 'jolly', as the gymkhana was often called, but by the 1880s it had become a regular feature of life under the British Raj. Its great virtue was that it was fun for everyone; male or female, if you could ride you could take part and, just as back home in England the village fête brought together every division of the social classes on equal terms, so in India did the gymkhana.

Troopers competed against officers; the senior officer's wife took on the newest recruit. In the stiff formality of British India, where life was filled with unwritten rules of behaviour and woe betide the unwary, it was rather nice to be able to let your hair down and relax.

Most regimental sports included gymkhana events of some kind. Many are recognisable today — musical sacks, bending, egg and spoon race — but there were others which called for a high degree of horsemanship and courage. Teams of mounted wrestlers, eight-strong, attempted to tip their opponents off their horses. Relay events often employed donkeys, mules, camels, traps, bicycles and native *tongas* as well as the Army remounts. Gymkhanas were good for morale, a change from route marches and drilling and great fun for those who, at polo tournaments and other events, were normally confined to the spectators' seats.

In those days, the games were usually played by adults. It was not until the 'gymkhana' (an Anglo-Indian derivation from 'gymnastics' and the Hindi word *gendkhana*, meaning ball-house or racquet court) was brought back to England by returning regiments that the scope of the sport was widened to allow children to take part. At first, mounted games were organised by cavalry regiments and polo clubs; later they were included in village horse shows. Here, the children's events tended to be of a fairly simple kind, requiring few assistants and the minimum of equipment. Adult classes were races, punctuated by sheep hurdles and generally held over a dangerously tight circuit only casually defined by a rope barrier. You had to be fast, tough and fearless to stand any chance of winning, and spills and thrills came in about equal measure.

Eventually, gymkhana organisers, alarmed by the high risk of accidents, started to devise games which called for skill and subtlety rather than sheer nerve. Hurdles were abolished and more stringent safety rules introduced. Today, gymkhanas are as safe for pony and rider as any sport involving horses can possibly be, yet because of the variety of events and the degree of horsemanship required the excitement they provoke is as intense as ever.

## THE GYMKHANA SITE AND ARENA

The best site for a gymkhana is a large, level field with easy access from a road for cars, trailers and horse boxes. For a show, the field ideally should have space to accommodate a ring or 'arena' big enough for all events to be held in safety, a collecting ring, an exercising arena, spectators' cars, horse boxes and trailers, horse lines, tents for the secretary, the judges and refreshments, and lavatories.

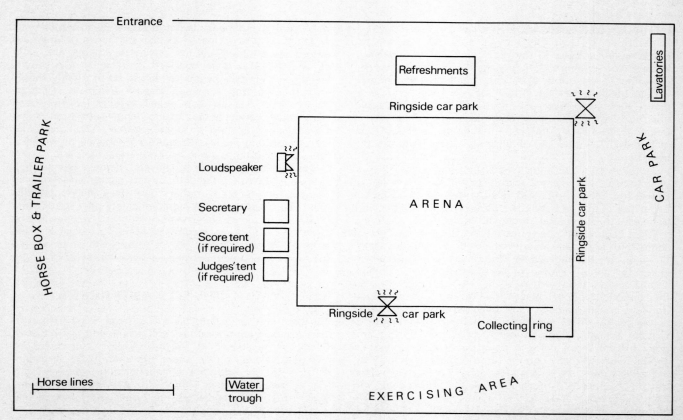

Entrance

Refreshments

Ringside car park

Loudspeaker

Secretary

Score tent
(if required)

Judges' tent
(if required)

ARENA

Ringside car park

Ringside car park

Collecting ring

Lavatories

CAR PARK

HORSE BOX & TRAILER PARK

Horse lines

Water trough

EXERCISING AREA

4

*Suggested layout for gymkhana field*

*The arena* requires posts and rope to define its boundaries. The entrance is normally through a roped-off section which is used as a collecting ring, with an optional separate exit nearby. Some shows with a varied programme of showing and jumping events may have a second ring where the gymkhana events are held.

The gymkhana ring should be roughly oblong in shape and measure at least 60 yards wide by 80 yards long. This gives room for a circle some 50 yards in diameter to be marked out within the arena for events such as musical wands or musical mats; this circle should be clearly defined by dressage cones, flags or straw bales. Other events can take place up and down the centre. These usually start and finish at the same point, and it helps the judges if the finishing line can be clearly marked with lawn whitening between shoulder-high flags at either end.

Events calling for the erection of posts (bending, potato race, etc.) are normally run in heats, with six competitors to a heat. This requires the provision of 36 posts. Each line of six posts should be six yards apart. The first posts should be put up some eight to ten yards from the start/finish line and the remainder at eight-yard intervals.

*The collecting ring* is the place where competitors gather when they are waiting to enter the ring. It is here that the steward in charge can separate the entrants into heats and keep the flow of events running smoothly. If space allows, it is wiser to have an arena exit away from the collecting ring. Outgoing competitors inevitably stop to talk to their friends and in the confusion it is difficult for the collecting ring steward to know which competitors have already competed and which are still awaiting their turn.

*The exercising arena* should occupy a little-used portion of the field about midway between the horse lines and horsebox park and the collecting ring. A practice jump may be set up here. The area is used to loosen up ponies after they have been unloaded from the horseboxes and to warm them up before an event.

*Spectators' cars* are best sited around the arena. Their presence helps to augment the rope barrier. If no ringside car parking is permitted, then a separate park must be provided.

*Horse boxes and trailers* do require a separate park, however, and should never be allowed at the ringside for fear of causing injury to bystanders. They are best placed at one side of the field, preferably not far from a water trough and certainly within earshot of loudspeaker announcements.

*Horse lines* are necessary as a base for those competitors who have hacked to the show. They should be in a sheltered spot and, like the horse boxes, near the water trough and loudspeaker calls. If there is no hedge or fence suitable for tying ponies to, specially erected lines will be needed.

*The secretary's office* is usually a tent, although an empty horse box or trailer makes a good substitute. It should be placed at the ringside, clearly labelled and equipped with table, chairs and, if possible, a blackboard or notice board.

*The judges* do not have to have a separate tent. Space can be reserved at the ringside for their cars or they can share the secretary's office. But wherever they are placed,

*Plan of arena*

6 rows of 6 bending poles, each pole 6-8 yds apart, each row 6-8 yds apart.

*Circle:* approx 50 yds dia. (This circle may be moved nearer the centre of the arena.)

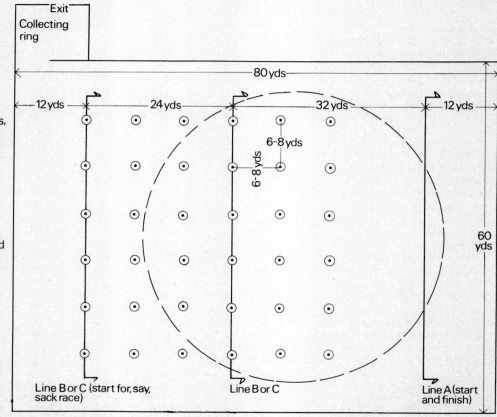

Exit
Collecting ring

80 yds

12 yds — 24 yds — 32 yds — 12 yds

6-8 yds

6-8 yds

60 yds

Line B or C (start for, say, sack race)

Line B or C

Line A (start and finish)

they should not be far from the secretary or organiser.

*Refreshments* may consist of orange squash and a bun or something much more elaborate. Either way, they should be under cover, near the spectators and within earshot of loudspeaker announcements. If the gymkhana field is near a farmhouse or public hall, it may be possible to arrange to use their cooking facilities (for tea, coffee and, possibly, soup). Otherwise, it could be necessary to lay on a large tent or marquee, complete with tables and folding chairs, and some means of heating water, such as calor gas stoves or urns.

*Lavatories* must be provided, suitably screened. Latrines may have to be dug or portable containers set up. Proximity to a public hall is, of course, the best answer. The lavatories should be clearly signposted.

*Equipment* for use in the ring (stakes, jumps, straw bales, apples, etc.) may be stacked near the secretary's office, from which stewards can collect them when necessary.

## THE IDEAL GYMKHANA PONY

In the gymkhana ring, a good little'un will nearly always beat a good big'un. Possibly this is one of the reasons why gymkhanas are so popular in Britain. These islands are unique in having no fewer than nine separate native breeds of pony, all of which have the true pony qualities — stamina, strength, surefootedness and agility. These are the qualities which the ideal gymkhana pony needs above all.

Temperamentally, he must be quick, intelligent and unflappable. The pony that spooks at flags, for example, or refuses to go near a plastic bucket, or balks at carrying a half-filled sack of hay, needs plenty of preliminary schooling at home. In much the same way as a police horse is trained to accept loud bangs, whistles, banners and jostling crowds, by constant repetition and lavish praise when things go right, so a gymkhana pony must be taught that no harm will come to him no matter what antics his rider chooses to perform.

The faults in conformation which would damn the pony in the show-ring need be no bar to gymkhana success. Who cares if he has a goose-rump or is a bit narrow in front as long as he can spring into a canter from a standing start and will stop on a halfpenny?

There are no hard and fast rules about the ideal age of a pony, although a young one lacks experience and an old one no longer has the speed. Nevertheless, there have been some very fine gymkhana ponies which were still top of their class when well into their twenties. Probably the best age is between ten and fifteen when he still has his strength, but many years of gymkhana competition have sharpened the pony's wits and taught him the wiles of the game.

## PRACTISING FOR A GYMKHANA

If you want your pony to become top-class in gymkhana events, the same rules apply as for any equestrian sport: practice and fitness. Practice should take place regularly and never for too long. Fitness comes from exercise and proper feeding.

*Getting a friend to help train your pony to lead*

A soft, fat, grass-fed pony will not be fit enough for fast, agile gymkhana work until you manage to turn some of the fat into muscle. This takes time and must be done gradually, starting, say, six weeks before the season begins with a daily routine of walking and jogging, leading to short bouts of extended trotting and cantering. At first, the pony may sweat up and get puffed, particularly if he is slow to lose his winter coat, and you should be careful not to overtax him at this stage. Slowly, however, his muscles will become less slack and the tendency to sweat will be reduced.

At the same time, give him additional concentrates to replace the energy he uses, so that he maintains his condition. If possible, put him in the stable for a few hours each day to prevent him from gorging himself on the new grass.

When schooling, concentrate on activities which will stand him in good stead in the gymkhana ring. Practise smooth, swift transitions between all the paces, using the voice as much as possible. In a gymkhana ring, it is unlikely that you will be allowed to carry a whip, so the pony must learn to respond promptly to leg aids. At home, these can be reinforced by a sharp tap with a stick, but remember to use the whip only as a means of correction. Do not flap your legs about — a pony's sides can quickly become deadened by constant kicking. Practise neck-reining — a pony which answers quickly to the movement of the reins will be saved from being hauled about or jabbed in the mouth.

Skill and agility at various paces are important. A slow collected canter is useful for events such as musical poles. For walk, trot and canter, the pony should be able to move

*Waving paper bags in your pony's face*

*Practising vaulting on to the pony's back*

swiftly at the selected pace without breaking, so practise lengthening the pace, then using the half-halt to bring him back almost to a walk before driving him on again. Never yank at the reins; the hand should resist without tugging and open as soon as you use your legs and seat to urge him on.

Spend some time teaching him to lead. Many events call for you to dismount and run along with the pony beside you. Having to drag a reluctant pony behind you is frustrating, and many otherwise skilled performances are spoilt by this annoying habit. A friend may be needed to help in overcoming the fault by encouraging the pony from behind. Always reward the pony when he does well; in the long run, the carrot is a thousand times better than the stick.

As the pony gets fitter and more responsive, he will improve in balance and co-operation. Before long, provided he is ridden calmly and sensibly, you will find that he starts to anticipate what is expected of him. By then he will be well on his way towards becoming an expert — and therefore more valuable — gymkhana pony.

You may still, however, have to get him used to the peculiar things which happen in gymkhana events. If he seems doubtful about music, for example, take a transistor into his field for short periods and gradually get him used to the curious sounds that come from it. Accustom him to rattling buckets, waving flags, flapping garments, even bursting balloons. Teach him to stay still while you mount and dismount. To have a pony which will stand like a statue as you vault on over his tail will gain valuable seconds in a race and may be the only efficient way of mounting a pillion passenger. Get him used to having you crawling between his legs. It is hopeless in an event like apple bobbing to have to worry about the pony's behaviour while you are chasing an elusive apple round a bucket of water.

## Useful Equipment at Home

*Bending poles* The best are six-foot stakes about the thickness of a broom handle, sharpened at one end so that they can be stuck into the ground. Broom handles themselves make very efficient practice poles. If you set them in empty paint pots, filled with cement, they will be stable and can be moved around easily. Vary the distance between the poles when practising because gymkhana organisers can be most idiosyncratic when it comes to setting them up. Remember that the closer you can turn round the last pole, the faster your time will be.

*Flags* Bamboo canes, borrowed from the garden shed, are useful for flags. The flag part can be cut out of old plastic fertiliser sacks, wrapped round one end of each cane and secured by staples.

*Buckets, bowls* Ordinary household ones will do, the gaudier the better. Practise throwing things into them, especially potatoes and tennis or ping-pong balls.

## Getting Yourself Fit

All the work spent in making the pony ready for gymkhanas will be wasted if you yourself are not fit. Useful exercises for this purpose are cycling, jogging, skipping and running on the spot. Ten to twenty minutes a day should be quite sufficient. If you are wise, you will also watch your weight — go easy on the roly-poly pudding and refuse that second helping of potatoes or bread and jam.

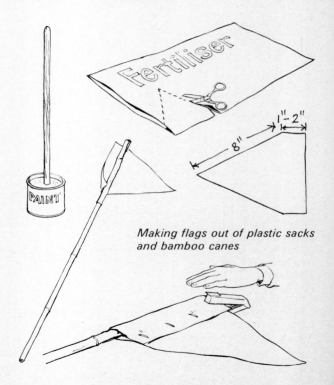

*Broom handles set in cement make very good bending poles*

*Making flags out of plastic sacks and bamboo canes*

## ENTERING AND PREPARING FOR A GYMKHANA

Once you have become a regular entrant at gymkhanas, it is likely that you will be sent schedules without having to apply. Until then, however, look out for posters advertising gymkhanas in the neighbourhood or watch for advertisements in the local newspaper. Larger shows, which may feature some gymkhana classes, usually advertise in *Horse and Hound*.

Most posters and advertisements give the name and address of the show secretary and an invitation to send an s.a.e (stamped, addressed envelope) for a schedule. When you apply, send a *sensible* envelope: there is nothing more infuriating for the hard-worked show secretary than to have to cram a large schedule into a tiny envelope fit only for notelets. Remember to apply for a schedule in plenty of time; many shows have a closing date for entries.

With most schedules, there is a separate entry form. This is usually divided into columns, in which you put down the classes you wish to enter (by number), the pony's name, owner's and rider's names and entry fee. There should also be a space at the bottom for entering your full name and address and possibly your age or date of birth. Money to cover the entry fees (cash, cheque or postal order) should be returned with the entry form to the secretary.

Take care to see that you abide by the closing date. Some gymkhanas charge double fees for late entries, some

allow late entries only if a class is not full and others will not allow late entries at all. In a few, usually small, gymkhanas, entries may only be made on the day.

The schedule should state clearly the different classes by name and details of eligibility. This may mean a height limit for the pony, age limit for the rider, or both. Sometimes there is a residential qualification.

## Horseville Gymkhana
### Entry Form

| Event No | Pony's Name | Owner's Name | Rider's Name | Entry Fee |
|----------|-------------|--------------|--------------|-----------|
| 2 | RUFUS | MRS E. SMITH | PENNY SMITH | 35p |
| 3 | " | " | " | 35p |
| 4 | " | " | " | 35p |
| 6 | SILVER | " | " | 35p |
| 8 | " | " | " | 35p |

Entrant's name PENNY SMITH    Total £1.75

Address THE LAURELS    Entrant's age 11

NEWTOWN, WESSEX

**Send entry form with money to Hon. Secretary, Ranch Farm, Horseville, Wessex, to arrive not later than August 4th.**

Once you have posted off your entries, nothing more is expected of you by the show secretary until the day itself.

A few days before the gymkhana, have your pony's feet checked and if necessary re-shod. This should not be left until the last minute.

## The Eve of the Gymkhana

This is the day for cleaning: yourself, your clothes, your pony, and your pony's tack.

*First, the pony:* exercise him lightly in the morning and devote the afternoon to getting him into spanking condition. Parts of a grey or any other light-coloured pony may need shampooing, particularly the tail and hind legs. Use soapflakes, washing-up liquid or a proprietary shampoo (not detergent in case it has an irritant effect) and rinse properly. Be particularly careful to dry the pony's heels. If you think you need the practice, plait the pony's mane, but do not leave the plaits in overnight. The mane may be damaged and the job will certainly have to be done again in the morning.

Some people like to keep a grass-fed pony in on the night before the gymkhana, mainly to save time in the morning if his field is some distance away or it is likely to rain. If this is your intention, keep the top half of the stable door wide open and fastened back and do not be tempted to put a rug on the pony. A pony accustomed to living out needs plenty of ventilation when he is in the stable.

*Second, the tack:* clean it thoroughly. This means taking the bridle to pieces and removing the girths and stirrups from the saddle. The bit and stirrup irons should be washed in hot water and dried carefully before being polished with metal polish. After putting metal polish on the bit, rinse it again and dry it on a tea towel. Brush the underside of the saddle with a stiff brush if the lining is made of linen or serge. Then work saddle soap into all leatherwork. Be careful not to use too damp a sponge — the soap should not lather. Wash nylon string girths and webbing girths in soapy water, using a nail brush if they are particularly dirty. Rinse and hang up to dry.

*Your own clothes:* since most stretch jodhpurs are machine-washable, there is no excuse nowadays for going to a gymkhana in grubby clothes. Unless you are entering a turn-out class as well as gymkhana events, there is no need to wear gloves or even a jacket, but your shirt (usually blue or white) should be clean and freshly ironed, your tie kept in place with a pin and any holes in your jersey neatly mended. Clean your riding or jodhpur boots and brush your hard hat. Put them out ready before you go to bed.

Last thing before bedtime, visit the stable and check that all is well, the pony's water bucket is full and that there is sufficient hay in his hay-net to keep him happy during the night.

## The Day of the Gymkhana

Whether you intend to hack to the gymkhana or to travel by horse box, always allow plenty of time before the moment of departure to get everything ready. The pony must be fed and watered and given time to digest his breakfast. He also needs grooming. You need time to change from your old jeans (worn, of course, when grooming) and to eat your own breakfast. If necessary, pack sandwiches, although most shows have refreshments available.

If you are hacking to the show, put on the pony's head-collar over his bridle after tacking up, knotting the rope loosely round his neck. Alternatively, buckle the halter round your waist.

Do not be late setting off. There is no point in exhausting the pony before you even arrive. Travel steadily. If the pony is fresh, it will not hurt him to work off some of the excess energy on the way, but try not to let him sweat up.

On arrival at the showground, make your way to the place allotted to pony lines and tie the pony up on his headcollar, loosen the girths and run up the stirrups. Go on foot to the secretary's tent, which should be clearly marked, to collect your competitor's number. Never take the pony to the tent — there is usually a crowd round the opening and you may have to wait your turn. The number will be for tying round your waist or your arm (according to the length of the tapes) and it is wisest to put it on straight away. Check with the secretary when your first event is likely to begin and half an hour beforehand take your pony to the exercising area to warm him up. This is particularly important if you come to the show by box.

Listen to the loudspeaker announcements. Competitors for each event are usually called for over the loudspeaker. When it is your turn, go to the collecting ring and wait quietly until the collecting ring steward tells you to enter the main ring.

Many events are organised in heats. If you are allotted

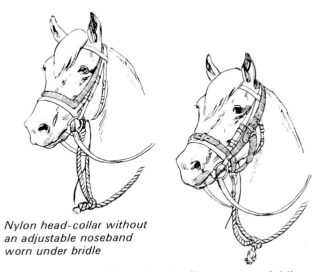

*Nylon head-collar without an adjustable noseband worn under bridle*

*Nylon head-collar worn over bridle with rope (attached by spring-clip to head-collar) knotted round pony's neck*

to a heat, do not argue even if all the other people in the heat are a great deal better and more experienced than you are. Your turn will come.

If you have any doubts about the rules for a particular event, ask the collecting ring steward while you are awaiting your turn. There may not be time to ask the starter and there is no point in complaining afterwards that you had no idea what to do.

Accept the judge's decisions cheerfully, even if you think you should have been given the verdict instead of someone else. The only time to query the judge's decision is when you know that a competitor is ineligible (because of her age or the height of her pony), in which case you should make the complaint in writing to the secretary and be prepared to pay a deposit of about £3. The deposit will be returned to you if the organisers, after investigating, uphold your complaint.

Do not dash out of the ring or gallop about madly between events. Seize every opportunity to rest your pony, dismounting and loosening the girths: the time you want him to use his energy is in the ring not out of it. If there is a long interval between your events, remove the saddle, but if the pony is hot and there is a breeze blowing, put your jacket or an old sack over his back to stop him from catching cold. From time to time take him to the water trough for a drink.

At the end of the day, try to find time to thank the organisers. It may seem a small thing, but a word of appreciation from the competitors is very gratifying to someone who has worked hard to make the day a success.

When you set off home, remember that the pony is tired too, so ride properly. Never slop along with loose reins, because a tired pony may stumble and fall. Always walk the last half-mile. Turn the pony out into his field straight away so that he can roll and get a drink. Rolling acts as a tonic to a field-kept pony. If he has an evening feed, give it to him thirty minutes to an hour later.

## The Day After

Next day is rest day for both you and your pony. But this does not mean ignoring him completely. Visit him in the field, catch him up and make a fuss of him. Then inspect him carefully to check that there is no heat or swelling in his legs.

After that you can make plans for the next show.

# GYMKHANA EVENTS

There is no official governing body for gymkhanas and no formal method of running any event. Variations are often found, according to the ingenuity and inventiveness of the organisers. However, over the years, a vague pattern of classes has emerged, some events being better established than others. The following list gives the most popular events, with a format which is widely used throughout the country. In all the instructions, the starting line, which is also the finishing line, is described as Line A. Line B, where the 'hazards' of the race are usually situated, should be between 30 and 60 yards from Line A.

## Anti-Litter Race (six in heat)

*Items needed* Litter (cartons, plastic tubs, cigarette packets etc.), allowing at least six items per competitor. Six bins, bowls or buckets. Six bamboo canes. Stop watch and whistle.

*Rules* Wait with a cane on Line A, next to your bucket. At the sound of the whistle, ride to Line B where litter is spread on the ground, and use your cane to pick up one item which you carry back to the bucket. Return for another item and so on until six pieces of litter have been collected.

*The winner* is the first rider to collect six items of litter and deposit them in his bucket. Alternatively, the rider who collects the most litter in a given time — say, 1 to 1½ minutes — wins the race. A blast on the whistle signifies that time is up.

*Note to organisers* This event is not suitable for a windy day!

## Apple-bobbing (six in heat)

*Items needed* Six bowls or buckets filled with water. One apple in each.

*Rules* Start on Line A. Ride to bowl on Line B, dismount and retrieve the apple from the water, using your teeth and without touching it with your hands. Remount and ride to finish.

*The winner* is the first to return with her apple still between her teeth. If the apple is dropped in transit, the rider may dismount and replace the apple in her mouth, this time using her hands, remount and carry on.

*Variation* Instead of placing the apple in a bowl of water, the organisers may suspend the apples on cotton from a clothes line stretched across Line B. 'No touching' rule still applies. This is sometimes called **Apple-picking** or **Bun-picking** if buns are used instead of apples.

## Ball and Basket Race (six in heat)

*Items needed* Four or six bending posts to each rider. Each post should have a container fixed to the top (old yoghurt cartons are suitable) with a tennis or rubber ball

in every container. Six laundry baskets on Line A.

*Rules* Start at Line A and collect each ball in turn, dropping it into the basket.

*The winner* is the first to have all four or six balls safely in the basket. If a ball is dropped or bounces out of the basket, the rider dismounts, retrieves ball, remounts and resumes race. The ball may be placed in the basket from the ground. It is the rider's responsibility to straighten the basket and retrieve the balls if the pony kicks the basket over.

## Ball and Racket Race (six in heat)

*Items needed* Row of bending poles for each rider. Six tennis rackets and balls.

*Rules* Start on Line A with ball balanced on racket. Bend up and down the poles without dropping the ball or touching it with the hand.

*The winner* is the first to finish. A dropped ball should be retrieved by the rider who may remount before replacing it on the racket.

## Balloon-bursting Race (six in heat)

*Items needed* Inflated balloons, allowing three to each rider, tied to tent pegs or skewers (have plenty of spares). Six bamboo canes, each with a pin taped to the end (lances). Peg the balloons to the ground at intervals between Lines A and B. Six posts on Line B.

*Rules* Ride to post on Line B, go round it and return to finish, bursting each balloon in turn with the lance as you go.

*The winner* is the first to finish.

## Barrel Elimination (no heats)

*Items needed* Eight to ten oil drums, laid end to end on their sides.

*Rules* Ride with the other competitors in a circle in single file, jumping the barrels when you come to them. After every rider has negotiated the obstacle once, one barrel is removed. Riders continue to jump in turn until only one barrel is left. If you run out or refuse, you are eliminated.

*The winner* is the last rider to clear the obstacle without fault.

*Note to organisers* There may be more than one rider at the end, who is able to negotiate the single barrel successfully. In this case, points may be awarded for style or the riders may share the prize.

## Bending (six in heat)

*Items needed* Six bending poles for each rider set in a straight line at eight-yard intervals.

*Rules* Start at Line A. Leaving the first pole on your right, weave in and out of the posts, round the end and back again.

*The winner* is the first to finish. If a post is missed, the rider must return to it and start again. A broken post means elimination.

## Brewer's Stakes (six in heat)

*Items needed* Six sets of false whiskers, six shirts or smocks, six scarves or handkerchiefs for use as neckerchiefs. Six tankards containing lemonade. All should be placed on Line B.

*Rules* Ride to Line B, dismount and don a shirt, neckerchief and whiskers. Drink the lemonade. Remount and ride to finish.

*The winner* is the first to arrive with brewer's dress intact.

## Bun Race (six in heat)

*Items needed* Six buns, placed on the ground at Line B.

*Rules* Ride to Line B, dismount and eat bun without touching it with the hand. Remount and ride to finish.

*The winner* is the first to finish.

## Button Race (six in heat)

*Items needed* Six buttons, six needles and thread held by six stewards, on Line B.

*Rules* Ride to steward and wait, mounted, while button is sewn to your sleeve. Ride to finish.

*The winner* is the first to cross the finishing line with the button still in place.

## Chase Me Charlie (no heats)

*Items needed* Two separate jumps, with poles which can be easily raised, set up on opposite sides of the arena. Stewards to man the jumps.

*Rules* Ride in procession over jumps, leaving sufficient room between you and the rider in front. A knock-down or refusal means elimination. After every rider has attempted both obstacles, the jumps are raised.

*The winner* is the one who completes every round successfully.

*Note to organisers* When the riders have been reduced to six, positions must be decided by allowing riders incurring faults to try again. Thus, if two riders knock down one

*Bending race*

**Dressing-up Race** (six in heat)
*Items needed* Articles of clothing for each rider, placed in a heap on Line B.
*Rules* Ride to Line B, dismount and put on garments. Remount and ride to finish.
*The winner* is the first to arrive with all garments properly put on.

jump on the same round, both should be allowed second attempts at the same height. If one then clears it she is placed fifth and the other rider sixth. If neither clears the jump, the prizes are shared.

*Note to organisers* Make certain that each rider's fancy dress is similar, and decide beforehand whether or not buttons have to be done up. Suitable items of dress include pyjamas, old shirts, cardigans, etc. If a hat is included, make it clear that the hat should be put on *over* the rider's own hat.

## Egg and Spoon Race (six in heat)

*Items needed* Six spoons, each containing a ping-pong or golf ball, on the ground at Line B.

*Rules* Ride to Line B, dismount and pick up spoon without touching the 'egg' with the hand. Lead pony to finish. If the 'egg' falls, you must scoop it up with the spoon.

*The winner* is the first to finish with the 'egg' still in its spoon.

## Flag Race (six in heat)

*Items needed* Eighteen flags (canes with pennants cut from old fertiliser sacks stapled to the ends – see figure on p. 18, stuck into six dressage cones on Line B. Allow three flags to each competitor. Six empty dressage cones on Line A. If cones are hard to come by, milk bottle crates may be used instead on Line B, but try to have cones on Line A.

*Rules* Start at Line A. Ride to Line B and collect a flag. Place it in the cone on Line A. Collect remaining flags in turn.

*The winner* is the first to have all three flags in the cone on Line A.

*Note to organisers* If the 'flag' part comes off the cane, this need not incur a penalty as the skill lies in getting the cane into the narrow neck of the cone.

*Concentration is essential in a flag race – and knotted reins are a precaution against entanglement*

## Hoop-La Race (six in heat)

*Items needed* Eighteen hoops (three for each competitor) about eight inches in diameter, placed on chairs or held by stewards on Line B. Six posts on Line A.

*Rules* Ride to chair or steward, collect one hoop and place it over post on Line A. Return for remaining hoops, one at a time.

*The winner* is the first to have three hoops over the post.

## Lead, Walk and Trot (no heats unless the entry is large)

*Items needed* None.

*Rules* Start dismounted and lead pony to a line midway between Lines A and B. Mount and walk to Line B. Trot back to Line A. If the pony breaks when either walking or trotting, the rider must stop, circle and continue.

*The winner* is the first to finish.

## Lucky Dip Race (six in heat)

*Items needed* Six bran tubs or cardboard boxes each containing sawdust and four small items, including a matchbox, set up on Line B.

*Rules* Ride to bran-tub, dismount and find matchbox. Remount and return to finish.

*The winner* is the first to arrive with a matchbox.

## Milliner's Race (six in heat)

*Items needed* Six sheets of newspaper, twelve pins. Six stewards to hold newspaper, pins and ponies on Line B.

*Rules* Ride to Line B, hand pony to steward and receive paper and two pins in exchange. Fashion hat out of newspaper, using pins to secure. Put hat on over your own hat, remount and ride to finish.

*The winner* is the first to arrive with hat intact.

*Note to organisers* Not suitable for a windy day.

## Musical Flags (no heats)

*Items needed* Coloured flags used to divide the perimeter of a circle into segments. The segments should be of different sizes. Hat containing coloured cards, corresponding to the coloured segments. Coloured balloons attached to posts may be used to mark the sectors instead of flags. Music.

*Rules* Ride round the outside of the circle to music. When the music stops, stand still. If you are beside a flag or balloon marking the boundary between two segments, move forward. The judge removes a card from the hat and calls out the colour. All riders caught in the corresponding sector are eliminated. Those left ride on when the music restarts. The game continues until all riders except one have been eliminated.

## Musical Mats (sometimes called Musical Sacks) (no heats)

*Items needed* Large circle, with a number of sacks scattered on the ground in the centre. There should be one sack fewer than the number of competitors. Music.

*Rules* Ride round perimeter of circle. When music stops, dismount *immediately* and lead pony to a mat or sack. Stand on the sack. If you cannot find a vacant sack, you are eliminated. The rest remount when the music starts again and ride on round the outside of the circle. The game continues, one sack being removed each time, until one rider (the winner) is left.

*Hastily dismounting for musical mats*

## Musical Mounting (no heats)

*Items needed* Large circle. Music.

*Rules* Ride round circle. When music stops, dismount, run round pony and remount from other side. Last up is eliminated. Continue until one rider (the winner) is left.

*Note to organisers* Decide beforehand which side the riders should dismount. This may be varied during the game.

## Musical Sacks (see Musical Mats)

## Musical Statues (no heats)

*Items needed* Large circle. Music.

*Rules* Ride round circle. When music stops, halt and stand perfectly still. Any pony or rider who moves before the music starts again is eliminated. Continue in this way until only one rider (the winner) is left.

*Note to organisers* Many riders and ponies will be eliminated to start with. Towards the end, very strict arbitration will be required. The advantage of this event is that it gives a chance of a prize to those children whose ponies are slow but steady and rarely win other events.

## Musical Wands (no heats)

*Items needed* Large circle. Posts (one less than the number of competitors) in the centre. Music.

*Rules* Ride round circle. When the music stops, ride to a post in the centre, stop and hold on to the post. Anyone failing to find a vacant post is eliminated. One post is removed each time and game continues until only one rider (the winner) is left.

*Note to organisers* It may be easier to have paper cups or cartons upturned on the posts. Competitors have to collect a cup when the music stops. When two riders are left (this applies whether cups are used or not), they should ride round in opposite directions. The steward in charge of the music should be asked to stop the music when both riders are approximately at the same point of the circle so that they race for the last post side by side. If they are on opposite sides, there is a risk of a head-on collision.

## Obstacle Race (may be run in heats if necessary)

*Items needed* These depend on the number and type of hazards which are introduced. Normally there should be about five hazards, set up around the arena in such a way that progression from one obstacle to the next is natural, there is no undue galloping and the competitors can readily understand the course.

A suitably hazardous course could be:

1 Balloon bursting. Balloons pegged to the ground. Canes with pins taped to the end.
2 Shoe shuffle. Pile of straw on the ground. As many pairs of old shoes as competitors, scattered among the straw.
3 Stepping stones. Five or six bricks, flowerpots, logs, etc., set in a row, two feet apart. Extra rows may be needed if there are a lot of competitors.
4 Channel crossing. Paper cups or child's sandals. Bamboo canes. Poles laid on the ground about ten yards apart.
5 Keep Britain Tidy. Buckets, litter (cartons, paper cups, etc.) scattered on ground. Litter bins or bins 15 yards further on.

*Rules* Start, holding cane, and ride to (1) row of balloons. Burst one and discard cane. Ride to (2), dismount, hand pony to steward and search in straw for matching pair of shoes. Remount, carrying shoes and ride to (3), dismount and, leading pony, walk along stepping stones. Discard shoes, remount and ride to (4). Take cane. Pick up paper cup or sandal on the end of the cane and ride across 'Channel' (space between two lines of poles). Discard cane and cup or shoe. Ride to (5), dismount and collect four pieces of litter in bucket. Run to litter bin, leading pony, and empty bucket into bin. Remount and ride to finish.

*The winner* is the first to finish, having completed all the tasks successfully.

*Note to organisers* Plenty of stewards should be at hand to see that each hazard is tackled properly. If, for example, a child falls off the stepping stones, she should return to the start of that obstacle and begin again. Be especially careful to check that four pieces of litter are collected.

## Polo Race (six in heat)

*Items needed* Six polo sticks. Six balls of different colours. Six posts erected on Line B.

*Rules* Start at Line A and use stick to hit ball to Line B, round post and back to finish.

*The winner* is the first to finish. Ball, stick, pony and rider must all cross the line.

## Postman's Chase (six in heat)

*Items needed* Six rows of four or six bending posts. Six envelopes weighted with sand on Line B. Six sacks.

*Rules* Carrying sack, ride in and out of bending posts to Line B. Dismount, pick up envelope and place in sack. Remount and carry sack between bending posts to finish.

*The winner* is the first to finish, complete with sack containing envelope.

## Potato Race (six in heat)

*Items needed* Six rows of six bending posts, each with a nail projecting from the top. Potatoes stuck on to the nails. Six buckets on Line A.

*Rules* Ride to last post, collect potato and return. Put potato in bucket. Continue collecting potatoes in turn until all six are in the bucket.

*The winner* is the first to have all six potatoes in the bucket.

*Note to organisers* The number of potatoes in each row can be reduced. Make it clear to competitors that if the potato misses the bucket or bounces out, or if the pony knocks the bucket over, they must dismount, place potato or potatoes in bucket and remount before continuing.

## Ribbon Race (six in heat)

*Items needed* Six rows of three posts. A length of ribbon or tape tied in a bow to each post.

*Rules* Start on Line A. Ride to first post, untie ribbon and ride on to second post. Collect ribbon and tie it to the first piece. Ride on and collect third ribbon, tying it to the other two. Ride back to finish.

*The winner* is the first to finish with all three pieces of ribbon securely tied together. Should they come undone when tugged, the competitor is disqualified.

**Run and Lead** (heats not necessary)
*Items needed* None.
*Rules* Ride to Line B, dismount and lead pony back to starting line.
*The winner* is the first to finish.

**Sack Race** (six in heat)
*Items needed* Six sacks laid on the ground at Line B.
*Rules* Ride to Line B. Dismount and get into sack. Leading pony, shuffle, jump or hobble to finish. Do not use the pony to support you while you run.
*The winner* is the first to arrive with her legs still in the sack.

**Saddling-up Race** (heats not necessary)
*Items needed* None, except that riders should remove their saddles and hand them to stewards who place them on Line B.
*Rules* Ride bareback to Line B, dismount and put on saddle. Mount and ride to finish.
*The winner* is the first to finish with all girth buckles done up and her feet in the stirrups.

**Shoe Scramble** (six in heat)
*Items needed* Pile of loose straw on Line B. Six pairs of shoes scattered in the straw. Six stewards.
*Rules* Ride to straw, dismount and hand pony to steward. Search in straw for matching pair of shoes, remount and ride to finish.
*The winner* is the first to finish with a proper pair of shoes.
*Note to organisers* This race can be made more difficult if the shoes are similar in style so that the competitors have to look for the size before being satisfied that they have a matching pair.

**Shopping Race** (no heats)
*Items needed* Nine shop signs — Butcher, Baker, Greengrocer, Grocer, Corn Chandler, Saddler, Chemist, Ironmonger, Fishmonger, for example — set around the arena. Nine stewards (shopkeepers) each with a pencil. Shopping lists written out on postcards, each bearing the names of six shops (every list should have a different order). Each competitor has a separate card. A steward (shopkeeper) stands beside each shop sign.
*Rules* Start from the centre of the arena and visit each of the six shops on your shopping list in turn, and in the order in which they are written down on your card. When the appropriate 'shopkeeper' has initialled your card, ride on to the next. As soon as your card is complete, go to the judge.
*The winner* is the first to reach the judge with a shopping card bearing six initials.
*Note to organisers* Tell steward that initials must be collected in order. If a rider arrives at the shop in the wrong order, the steward should not initial the card but direct the competitor to the right shop.

**Stepping Stones** (six in heat)
*Items needed* Six rows of stepping stones (bricks, flowerpots, logs, etc.) set up at two-foot intervals midway between Lines A and B. Six posts on Line B.

*Rules* Ride to stepping stones, dismount and walk along them, leading pony. Remount, ride round post on Line B and back to stepping stones. Dismount again, negotiate stones, remount and ride to finish.

*The winner* is the first to finish, having walked across the stepping stones in both directions without knocking them over or touching the ground.

*Note to organisers* If the rider falls off the stepping stones or for any reason fails to negotiate them properly, she must return and cross them all again.

## Supermarket Snatch (six in heat)

*Items needed* Several piles of articles, all the articles in the same pile being identical. Six shopping bags. Suitable articles are: tins of saddle soap, hoofpicks, ribbons, paper mugs, packets of soap powder, potatoes, socks, matchboxes weighted with stones, apples, dusters. The piles should be dotted around the arena and placed at different levels, so that riders have to dismount to collect some. Ribbons, for example, could be tied to a post, matchboxes placed on an oil drum, socks in a box on a chair.

*Rules* Start with a shopping bag and ride to each pile in turn, collecting one article. Articles may be collected in any order.

*The winner* is the first to return to the starting line with a shopping bag containing one of each item.

## Thread and Needle Race (six in heat)

*Items needed* Six stewards on Line B, each with a needle and piece of cotton.

*Rules* Start on Line A. Ride to steward. Dismount and thread cotton into needle. Remount and return to finish.

*The winner* is the first to finish with the cotton still threaded through the needle.

## Unsaddling Race (six in heat)

*Items needed* None.

*Rules* Ride to Line B, dismount and remove saddle, running up the stirrups first. Remount and ride bareback to finish.

*The winner* is the first to finish.

## V.C. Race (six in heat)

*Items needed* Six sacks, loosely filled with straw or hay, tied with string at the neck and round the middle, and placed in a row on Line B.

*Rules* Ride to Line B, collect 'body' (sack of straw), place it across the pony's withers and ride to finish.

*The winner* is the first to finish with the rescued 'body' still across the pony's withers.

## Walk, Trot and Canter (no heats necessary)

*Items needed* An extra line, C, midway between Lines A and B. The line should be clearly defined either by stewards or by flags.

*Rules* Walk to Line C, trot to Line B and gallop to finish. If the pony breaks at the walk or trot, circle once and continue.

*The winner* is the first to finish.

*Note to organisers* Ponies breaking into a faster pace must be turned round immediately, on pain of disqualification. If no galloping is preferred, the race can become simply a

**Walk and Trot,** in which case Line C is not needed, the transition coming at Line B. Alternatively, the paces can be taken in reverse order, i.e. **Canter, Trot and Walk.** The rules for breaking, however, remain the same.

# TEAM AND PAIRS EVENTS

### Relay Races

Many of the foregoing events can be run as relay races for teams of, say, four. Each team should wear different coloured bands and be provided with a baton. Members line up behind the starting line and at the word 'Go' the first member of each team completes the allotted tasks before returning to hand over the baton to the next member, this continuing until the whole team has competed.

The following events are most suitable for teams: Apple-bobbing (organisers should see that there are enough apples in each bowl for all members of the team); Ball and Racket Race; Bending; Bun Race (extra buns are needed); Egg and Spoon Race (team members can hand over the spoon with its 'egg' to the next member, or additional eggs and spoons will have to be provided; if the former course is decided upon, it would help to have half the team at Line A, the other half at Line B and to start the race with the first rider holding the egg and spoon: members would remain mounted throughout); Lead, Walk and Trot; Lucky Dip (with plenty of matchboxes); Milliner's Race (with extra newspaper and pins); Postman's Chase (allowing four envelopes for each team – the sack can be passed from one competitor to the next); Run and Lead; Sack Race (in this, the second team member gets into the sack and leads pony to Line B, leaves sack on the ground and rides back to third member who completes the course in a similar fashion to the first member of the team. This race is best run with an odd number in each team); Saddling-up Race; Stepping Stones; Thread the Needle (with extra needles and thread); Unsaddling Race; and Walk, Trot and Canter.

### Pairs Events

Mounted games and gymkhana events are primarily a means of relaxation and fun. In riding schools, where most of the riding is instructional, the proprietors often find that the occasional change from 'work' is marvellously beneficial to instructors, ponies and pupils alike. The problem is that usually there are not enough ponies to go round all the riders who want to take part. The following events should go some way towards solving this problem as each requires only one pony to every two riders. In each case it is assumed that there will be six pairs to a heat.

### Aunt Sally

*Items needed* Six dressage cones with a beach ball balanced on each one, set up about twelve feet behind Line B. Six buckets containing beanbags on Line B. Partners wait, dismounted, beside the buckets.

*Rules* Start on Line A and ride to partner. Dismount, handing pony to partner and, standing at Line B, try to knock the beach ball off the cone with the beanbags. As

soon as the ball falls, remount and with partner as pillion passenger ride to finish.
*The winners* are the first pair to arrive.

### Button Stitching
*Items needed* Six buttons and six needles and thread, held by partner at Line B.
*Rules* Ride to partner and stand while she sews the button to the rider's sleeve. Ride to finish, either alone or with partner as passenger.
*The winner* is the first back at the starting line.

### Gretna Green
*Items needed* Six curtain rings, six notepads and pencils, placed on chairs at Line B. Partners wait in a row midway between Lines A and B.
*Rules* Ride to partner, dismount and help partner on to pony. Get up behind partner and ride pillion to Line B. Both dismount, partner puts on ring and both sign register. Both remount and, riding pillion, return to finish.
*The winners* are the first pair home.
*Note to organisers* If pillion riding is felt to be unsafe because the riders or ponies are inexperienced, the first rider can lead her partner. This is quite a good event for beginners, who can be teamed up with older, more experienced riders.

### Laundry Race
*Items needed* Clothes line erected across Line B, carrying 18 items of clothing (socks, handkerchiefs, vests, etc.). Six laundry baskets. Partners should wait at Line B.

*Rules* Carrying basket, ride to Line B. Hand basket to partner and dismount. Hold pony while partner unpegs three articles of clothing and puts them in basket. Help partner on to pony, hand her the basket. Partner rides to finish, carrying basket.
*The winner* is the first to return, carrying a full basket. If any clothing drops out on the way, the dismounted partner may run and retrieve it while her partner waits.

### Musical Mats (no heats)
*Items needed* Large circle, with mats scattered about in the centre. Partners stand on the mats. Music.
*Rules* Partner 1 rides pony round circle. When music stops, she dismounts and, leading pony, runs into the centre to join Partner 2 on the mat. She helps Partner 2 on to the pony. The last one up is out. Partner 2 then rides round while Partner 1 stays in the centre.
*The winners* are the last pair left in.

### Rescue Race
*Items needed* Short lengths of tape or rope. Partners sit on the ground at Line B with their ankles and wrists tied.
*Rules* Ride to partner, dismount and release the 'prisoner'. Help partner on to pony and lead pony back to finish.
*The winners* are the first pair home, with the captive untied and the reins over the pony's neck and held by the captive.

### Shirt Race
*Items needed* Six voluminous shirts without buttons. Partners on Line B.

*Rules* Before starting, put on shirt. Stand beside pony. At signal, mount and ride to Line B. Dismount, and remove shirt which is then donned by partner. Partner mounts and rides to finish.
*The winner* is the first home.

## Wheelbarrow Race

*Items needed* Six wheelbarrows, held by partners on Line B.
*Rules* Ride to Line B, dismount and help partner into wheelbarrow. With partner leading pony, wheel her back to the starting line.
*The winners* are the first pair to finish.

## LEADING REIN CLASSES

Many gymkhanas include a section for beginners whose ponies must be led. Usually, the section is limited to children aged, say, eight and under, and these children are not allowed to take part in any other events in the show. This is intended to prevent a precocious rider, who qualifies by age for the leading rein classes, from winning all the beginners' events and then going on to take many other prizes in older sections. The leading rein classes are held solely to encourage the young beginner.

Although most of the events already described can be adapted for riders on the leading rein, it is best if possible

*The leading rein class – a chance for the novice rider*

to choose events which involve the rider and do not simply test the fitness and speed of the handler! The Bending Race, for example, can be won by a child who has never been on a pony before if the pony leads well and the handler runs fast. The same applies to Walk and Trot.

From the safety point of view, try to avoid a situation where dismounted children and ponies (even those controlled by handlers) are milling around together. The heels of a kicking pony are just at head-height to little children. Rules for events such as Egg and Spoon or Sack Race, therefore, should stipulate that the handlers stay with the ponies while the children set off for the winning post alone, and the winner is the first *child* across the line. Two excellent events for leading rein candidates are as follows:

### Crossing the River (no heats)

*Items needed* Large circle, with two segments ('rivers') about ten yards wide marked off by jumping poles laid on the ground. Music.

*Rules* Competitors ride round the outside of the circle. When the music stops, any riders caught in the 'rivers' are out.

*The winner* is the last child left in.

*Note to organisers* This is a good event for placing at the end of a leading rein section, especially where the object is to send every child home with a rosette. Invariably, there will be one or two children who carry off all the prizes in the other leading rein classes: a little judicious 'arranging' by the person controlling the music can ensure that these children are the first to be elimi ated in Crossing the River!

### Musical Mats (no heats)

*Items needed* Large circle with sacks scattered on the ground in the centre. Music.

*Rules* Riders are led round the perimeter of the circle. When the music stops, they dismount and run to a mat, while the handlers remain on the outside of the circle with the ponies. Any child failing to find a vacant mat is eliminated. One sack at a time is removed.

*The winner* is the last child left in.

## GAMES FOR THE DISABLED RIDER

Riding is now a widely acknowledged therapy for both the physically disabled and the mentally handicapped. Children especially derive tremendous confidence from their relationship with a horse or pony and look forward eagerly to their regular riding lessons.

Not surprisingly, they also enjoy games, and many of the events already described can be adapted to allow for the riders' disabilities.

Events which are particularly suitable are those in which the rider has only to sit on the pony: for example, Bending, Walk and Trot or Crossing the River. Other popular events are Musical Wands and Musical Mats, in which the handler leads the pony into the centre of the circle and grasps the pole or stands on the mat. In a Dressing-up Race, choose such items of clothing as hats, mufflers and neck-ties which can be put on the competitor by the assistants if the child is unable to dress herself/himself.

Many gymkhanas nowadays include events open only

*A young spastic child preparing to take part in a 'Riding for the Disabled' event*

to the disabled. The most successful are those which are interspersed with the ordinary events on the programme rather than those placed in a separate section. For the handicapped riders taking part, the fun lies not only in competing but also in mingling with the other children — in the collecting ring and round the ringside. The intervals between their events give them some rest and allow them to watch and cheer on their friends. For a time, they cease to be any different from the other children, and this, of course, is the best therapy of all.

## GENERAL RULES

In spite of there being no governing body, most gymkhanas do in fact conform to a set of general rules, which may or may not be set out in the schedule. If you assume that the following rules apply whatever gymkhana you attend, you are unlikely to go far wrong.

1 No rider and/or pony may enter more than once in any one event.
2 Whips and spurs may not be used.
3 Hard hats must be worn at all times, unless the conditions for any class decree otherwise.
4 No pony which is unfit through age or condition will be allowed to take part.
5 Ponies must be properly fitted with saddles and bridles, except where individual classes state otherwise.
6 Riders may not enter or wait in the ring except when taking part in an event, or unless they have been invited to do so by the judge.

7 Unruly ponies, which are not under control, may be turned out of the ring by the judge. Ponies which kick may also be eliminated.
8 Riders may be given assistance from stewards or spectators only at the discretion of the judge.
9 Rough, dangerous riding and bad behaviour, both inside and outside the ring, may lead to disqualification from the whole gymkhana.
10 Reins may not be looped under the pony's neck at any time. Feet must be in the stirrups unless the conditions of a class deem otherwise.
11 The organisers may alter the running order of the programme or cancel an event at their discretion. The judge may similarly change the rules for an event, or order a part or all of it to be run again.
12 If a rider withdraws from an event, for whatever reason, entry money will be refunded only at the organiser's discretion.
13 The judge's decision is final.
14 A formal complaint must be made within half-an-hour of the alleged offence having occurred. It must be made in writing to the organiser and accompanied by a deposit of £3, refundable if the complaint is upheld.

**Disclaimer**
Most schedules will display a disclaimer of liability for injury incurred during the gymkhana, usually set out along these lines: 'The organising committee does not accept any liability for any accident, damage, injury or illness to horses, owners, riders, spectators, ground, or any other person or property whatever.'

However, should you or your pony suffer an injury while competing in the show, especially if it can be proved to have been due to negligence on the part of the organisers, it is worth taking legal advice to see if there is any possibility of making a claim for compensation or damages. Supposing, for example, that your pony were to trip over a mallet or similar object which had been carelessly left in the ring by one of the stewards, this might well be regarded as reasonable grounds for compensation.

Wise gymkhana organisers, therefore, usually insure themselves against claims arising under two forms of liability:

1 Public Liability, which is legal liability for bodily injury and/or damage to the property of third parties caused through the fault or negligence of themselves or their servants in connection with the gymkhana.

2 Contractual Liability, which is liability accepted under a contract or agreement and applies if the gymkhana is held on land, such as a public park, which is normally open to the general public.

## THE PRINCE PHILIP CUP

In 1957, His Royal Highness the Duke of Edinburgh presented a challenge cup for a Mounted Games Championship to be competed for annually by members of the Pony Club. With this gesture, gymkhana events were lifted out of the realm of purely local and often haphazard affairs.

The Pony Club, an internationally recognised youth organisation, has a membership in Great Britain of 50,000, with a further 65,000 in branches and affiliated societies overseas. The Championship provided local organisers with an incentive to raise and train teams of young riders and their ponies to a new pinnacle of horsemanship.

The national finals of the Prince Philip Cup, as the Championship is often called, are held at the Horse of the Year Show in October each year between teams of five children from six Pony Club branches. To reach Wembley, each team must have won a zone final at which the winners and runners-up of various area finals were competing.

Every day at the Horse of the Year Show, the finalists take part in a variety of gymkhana events, all hoping to amass enough points during the week to win the coveted challenge cup on the last night.

By and large, the events are exactly the same as those held at the smallest gymkhana anywhere in the country during the summer season. The difference lies in the exceptional skill of the ponies and the agility of their riders.

# DO'S AND DON'TS FOR
# GYMKHANA ORGANISERS

**Do . . .**

- Order rosettes and numbers and book the loudspeaker equipment in plenty of time.
- Enter the names of competitors under the appropriate classes in the entry book as soon as the entry forms arrive. There is never enough time to catch up on these tasks nearer the day.
- Arrange for your most authoritative friends to act as collecting ring steward and senior judge. Argumentative competitors need a firm hand!
- See that there are enough stewards in the ring. Where, for example, six rosettes are awarded, there should be one person to watch for the winner, one to watch for the second, one for the third, and so on. A single judge cannot possibly hope to separate all six places in a tight finish without a mistake.
- Remember to visit the bank for small change so that gate stewards and tea helpers can start the day with an adequate float.
- Set the ring up and deliver all equipment to the ground one or two days before the show date.
- Be on the ground at least one hour before the gymkhana begins.
- Sort out the rosettes and prizes for each event well in advance, so that they are ready for handing to the judge's steward at the start of each class.

**Don't . . .**

- Put a leading rein best rider class at the beginning of the day and the rest of the leading rein class at the end. It is better to group all leading rein classes together, generally at the start of the show, so that little ones can be taken home before they and their ponies get fractious.
- Expect to see very much of the gymkhana yourself, even if your own child is competing.
- Accept any invitation for the evening of the show. You will be the first to arrive at the start of the day: and certainly the last to leave.
- Allow the gymkhana to over-run. It is better to close a class, telling late entrants that the event is now full, than still to be carrying on when dusk has fallen.
- Be upset by rude or bad-tempered competitors or — more likely — competitors' parents. If they leave in high dudgeon, be glad: you are better off without them.
- Panic. Problems can be sorted out quickly if the organiser stays calm and uses the loudspeaker to give the reasons for any delay.
- Forget that the loudspeaker is at your disposal. If you need a particular person urgently, put the request out over the microphone.
- Forget to thank everyone for helping. You will need their assistance in the future — if you can ever face running a gymkhana again.